2016

THE BIGGEST
UPSETS
OF ALL TIME

THE LEGENDARY
WORLD OF SPORTS

BY BARRY WILNER

SportsZone
An Imprint of Abdo Publishing | abdopublishing.com

abdopublishing.com

Published by Abdo Publishing, a division of ABDO, PO Box 398166, Minneapolis, Minnesota 55439. Copyright © 2016 by Abdo Consulting Group, Inc. International copyrights reserved in all countries. No part of this book may be reproduced in any form without written permission from the publisher. SportsZone™ is a trademark and logo of Abdo Publishing.

Printed in the United States of America, North Mankato, Minnesota
082015
012016

THIS BOOK CONTAINS
RECYCLED MATERIALS

Cover Photo: Ben Liebenberg/AP Images
Interior Photos: Ben Liebenberg/AP Images, 1; AP Images, 4, 7, 8, 10, 14, 17, 19, 20, 22, 24, 26; Vernon Biever/AP Images, 13; Rusty Kennedy/AP Images, 28; Bob Galbraith/AP Images, 30; Katsumi Kasahara/AP Images, 33; Ross D. Franklin/AP Images, 34; Ted S. Warren/AP Images, 36; David Duprey/AP Images, 38; Elaine Thompson/AP Images, 40; Charlie Neibergall/AP Images, 43; Nigel Kinrade/Autostock/AP Images, 45

Editor: Patrick Donnelly
Series Designer: Nikki Farinella

Library of Congress Control Number: 2015945543

Cataloging-in-Publication Data
Wilner, Barry.
  The biggest upsets of all time / Barry Wilner.
     p. cm. -- (The legendary world of sports)
  ISBN 978-1-62403-988-1 (lib. bdg.)
  Includes bibliographical references and index.
  1. Sports upsets--Juvenile literature.   I. Title.
  796.09--dc23

2015945543

TABLE OF CONTENTS

4

1919 SANFORD STAKES
UPSET PULLS THE UPSET

An upset is an unexpected result in a contest. And there have been few more fitting examples of an upset than the 1919 Sanford Stakes. That day a horse named Upset pulled off one of the biggest surprises in sports history.

Everybody expected an easy win for Man o' War. The undefeated two-year-old horse faced a good but not great field in the six-furlong race at Saratoga Race Course in New York. Man o' War had won all six of his races. He was already being called the greatest racehorse in America, even though it was still his first season. And he had beaten Upset on the same track at the same distance 11 days earlier.

Upset, *right*, holds off Man o' War down the stretch at the 1919 Sanford Stakes.

But Man o' War was in trouble from the start. Actually, trouble started even earlier—the regular starter for the races was absent. In the days before starting gates, the horses lined up behind a mesh tape at the starting line. But the replacement starter had problems settling the horses. Man o' War acted up so much that he was standing sideways and flat-footed when the race started. Every other horse took off down the track. Man o' War had lots of chasing to do.

With jockey Johnny Loftus riding his horse hard, Man o' War caught every horse except Upset. As they closed in on the finish line, Man o' War was within a half-length of passing Upset. Too late: Upset scored the huge upset.

Man o' War ran 21 races in his career. He won 20 of them. Upset was the only horse to get the best of him.

Man o' War won 20 of 21 races in his career.

JUNHO DE 1950

BRASIL

8

2

1950 WORLD CUP
COLONIAL UPRISING

The United States was not exactly a soccer power in 1950. Few US sports fans even knew the team was playing in that year's World Cup in Brazil. Meanwhile, soccer was wildly popular in England. And the English team was a favorite to win the World Cup.

The US team had lost its first game. England needed a win to keep alive its hopes of advancing. And the English took charge right away, firing shot after shot at US keeper Frank Borghi. But Borghi stood firm and stopped them all.

Just before halftime, US captain Walter Bahr launched a ball from 25 yards (23 m) out. England

The 1950 World Cup program

Fans carry Joe Gaetjens off the field after the shocking US upset of England in the 1950 World Cup.

keeper Bert Williams was ready for an easy save. But before the ball got to Williams, American Joe Gaetjens dived, put his head on it, and sent it into the net.

Hardly anyone could believe it. Surely England would storm back, and the US lead would be a distant memory. Except that England could not get one past Borghi. The English kept the ball in the US part of the field for almost the whole second half. But the 1–0 lead held up. When it was over and the Americans had won, they carried off Gaetjens on their shoulders.

"If we played them the next day," Borghi said, "they'd probably beat us 10–0."

FRENCH FLOP

France had won the 1998 World Cup on home soil. Four years later, it was one of the favorites in the 2002 World Cup. But in its opening match, Senegal—a team not known for its defense—shut out the mighty French team. Papa Bouba Diop scored the only goal in Senegal's 1–0 stunner.

3

1969 SUPER BOWL

JOE, JETS CLIP COLTS

The first Super Bowl was played after the 1966 season. The winner of the National Football League (NFL) faced the champion of the American Football League (AFL). The AFL had only been around since 1960. Most people thought the NFL was the better league. The NFL's Green Bay Packers seemed to back that up by winning the first two Super Bowls.

Then came Super Bowl III. The NFL champion Baltimore Colts were 18-point favorites against the AFL champion New York Jets. Even so, Jets quarterback Joe Namath said that his team would win. He not only said it. He guaranteed it. Namath's teammates backed him up.

The Jets' Matt Snell follows a block from teammate Bill Mathis, *31*, in the fourth quarter of Super Bowl III.

Nobody had run the ball well against Baltimore that year. The Jets did. Bruising running back Matt Snell carried the ball 30 times for 121 yards. He also scored on a 4-yard touchdown run. Kicker Jim Turner made three field goals, and the Jets led 16–0.

The Colts' offense sputtered. New York intercepted three passes in the first half. A last-gasp touchdown was all that Baltimore could manage. New York shocked the football world with a 16–7 win. Namath jogged off the field waving his right index finger in the air. It symbolized what he knew all week—that his Jets were number one.

4

1969 WORLD SERIES
THE AMAZIN' METS

T he New York Mets had been anything but amazing. They began play as a Major League Baseball (MLB) expansion team in 1962. In their first year they won 40 games and lost 120. They finished last in the National League (NL) five times in their first seven seasons.

But all that changed in 1969. Suddenly the lovable losers became winners. Armed with strong young pitchers Tom Seaver and Jerry Koosman, they began to get people out. Clutch hitters Cleon Jones and Tommie Agee led the offensive attack. Fans began referring to them as "The Amazin' Mets."

Ace right-hander Tom Seaver won a career-high 25 games for the New York Mets in 1969.

In September the Mets rallied past the Chicago Cubs to win their division. They had been 100-to-1 shots to win the NL East. But the winning did not stop there. New York then swept three straight games from the Atlanta Braves in the NL Championship Series.

The mighty Baltimore Orioles, champions of the American League (AL), awaited them in the World Series. The Mets were huge underdogs. But they believed their pitchers would shut down the Baltimore lineup. And they did. Orioles stars Frank Robinson and Brooks Robinson were a combined 4-for-35 at the plate in the series.

The Mets played loose and confident. They pitched well, got big hits, and made great catches. After losing Game 1, they swept the next four. The lovable losers ended the year on top of the baseball world. What could be more *amazin'* than that?

New Yorkers embraced the Amazin' Mets during their magical run to the 1969 World Series.

5

1971 STANLEY CUP
DRYDEN'S DEBUT

The Montreal Canadiens dominated the National Hockey League (NHL) in the 1950s and 1960s. But in the spring of 1971 they were supposed to go down quietly in the first round of the Stanley Cup playoffs. Their opponent, the Boston Bruins, seemed unstoppable.

Led by Bobby Orr and Phil Esposito, the Bruins had set numerous NHL records. They went 57–14–7 that season. Their 121 points were 12 more than any other team and 24 more than the Canadiens' total. They almost never lost at home. And in the week before the playoffs, the Bruins had beaten Montreal 6–3 and 7–2.

But Montreal had a secret weapon. Rookie goalie Ken Dryden had played in only six NHL games. People

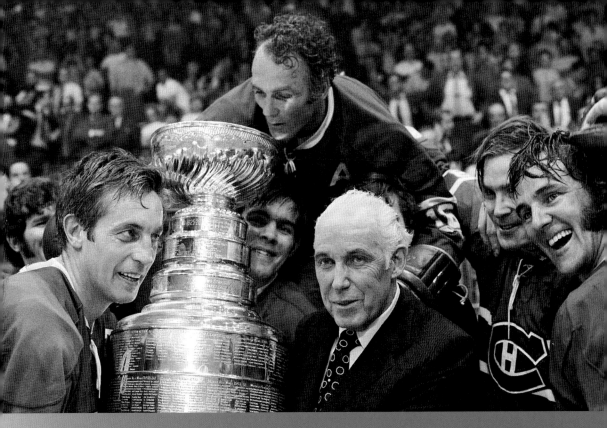

The Canadiens' first-round upset of Boston led to a win over Chicago in the Stanley Cup Finals.

expected him to be a sitting duck in the net. Instead, as Esposito later said, Dryden was more like an octopus. He made dozens of amazing saves. Before Game 7, Dryden said he was nervous. But the nerves disappeared when he took the ice. He allowed only two goals as Montreal won 4–2. A month later, the Canadiens won the Stanley Cup. And Dryden was named the Most Valuable Player (MVP) of the playoffs.

6

1980 WINTER OLYMPICS
MIRACLE ON ICE

"**U**-S-A! U-S-A!"

The hockey arena at Lake Placid, New York, shook with patriotic chants. On the ice, a bunch of amateurs in star-spangled uniforms mobbed one another. They had pulled off one of the most shocking upsets in sports history.

The 1980 US Olympic hockey team was not supposed to contend for a medal. Coach Herb Brooks had built a squad full of college kids. Their job? Defeat the four-time defending champion Soviet Union.

Once the Olympics began, so did the miracles. Team USA trailed Sweden 2–1 in the final minute of their Olympic opener. Brooks pulled goalie Jim

Herb Brooks pushed all the right buttons as he coached Team USA to the gold medal at the 1980 Winter Olympics.

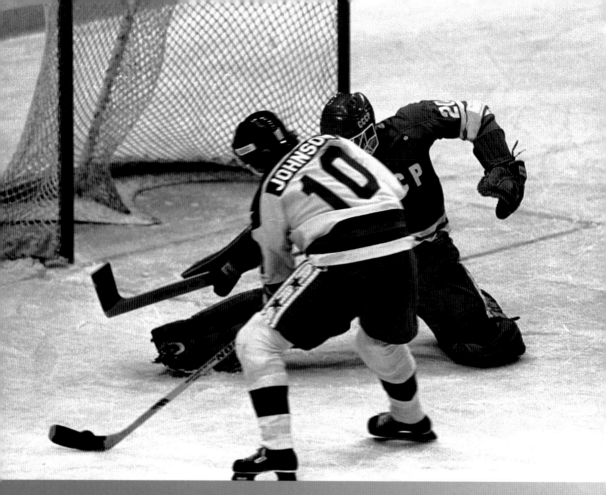

US forward Mark Johnson beats Soviet goalie Vladislav Tretiak for a goal in the first period of Team USA's stunning victory.

Craig for an extra skater. With 27 seconds left, Bill Baker rifled a slap shot past Sweden goalie Pelle Lindbergh. The tie gave them an important point in the pool standings.

Baker's goal provided a spark. The Americans began playing up to their potential. They won their next four games, including a 7–3 win against the powerful Czechs. Shockingly the kids from the United States were in the medal round. Their first game was against the Soviets.

The Americans trailed three times. But they countered each Soviet goal with one of their own. Mark Johnson's second goal of the night tied it with 12 minutes remaining. Two minutes later, Mike Eruzione fired a shot that found the back of the net. The goal put the USA on top 4–3.

In the final minutes, Craig and the Americans were holding on. ABC announcer Al Michaels counted down the last few seconds. Then he made a call for the ages: "Do you believe in miracles? Yes!"

USA 4, Soviet Union 3. Two days later, the Americans beat Finland. The gold medal was theirs.

7

1983 NCAA TOURNEY
WOLFPACK'S WILD WIN

Jim Valvano ran around the court, looking for somebody to hug. The North Carolina State basketball coach was not prepared for a big celebration. After all, it was the championship game of the 1983 National Collegiate Athletic Association (NCAA) tournament. And his team was supposed to have lost early in the tournament.

The Wolfpack barely made the NCAA field. They won their conference tourney to get in. But that was all the opening they needed. As the sixth seed in the West regional, they beat Pepperdine in double overtime, then upset third-seeded Nevada, Las Vegas, by a point. They rolled past Utah in the Sweet 16.

Lorenzo Charles slams home the game-winning basket in North Carolina State's upset of Houston in 1983.

Jim Valvano, *center*, is carried off the court after his Wolfpack knocked off heavily favored Houston to win the 1983 NCAA basketball title.

Then they nipped top-seeded Virginia 63–62 to reach the Final Four.

In the national semifinals, North Carolina State knocked off Georgia. That put the Wolfpack in the national championship game. They faced Houston, the number one team in the nation. The Cougars' wide-open, dunk-crazy offense earned a unique nickname: Phi Slamma Jamma.

It looked like the end of the line for the Wolfpack. With 10 minutes remaining, they trailed by seven points. The Cougars, led by first-team All-Americans

Akeem "The Dream" Olajuwon and Clyde Drexler, were too fast and strong.

But the Wolfpack came back. They rallied to tie the game. Then they got the ball with 44 seconds left. Valvano told his team to play for one last shot. Houston played strong defense, though. Guard Dereck Whittenburg's 35-foot (11-m) heave fell short.

But the ball landed in the hands of teammate Lorenzo Charles. He dunked it, the buzzer sounded, and the Wolfpack had a stunning victory.

ISLAND SURPRISE

On December 23, 1982, top-ranked Virginia and superstar center Ralph Sampson visited Hawaii to play tiny Chaminade. The Silverswords, whose own center was nearly a foot shorter than Sampson, shocked the world with a 77–72 win.

8

1988 WORLD SERIES

GIBSON GOES DEEP

Kirk Gibson limped to home plate in the ninth inning of Game 1 of the 1988 World Series. The Los Angeles Dodgers star had injured his knees and hamstrings. He could barely stride into a pitch, let alone run the bases or play the field. He was not even in uniform when the ninth inning began.

Dennis Eckersley of the Oakland Athletics stared down Gibson. Eckersley was the toughest relief pitcher in his era. He had been called on to protect a 4–3 lead. Eckersley had already gotten the first two outs. Then he walked Mike Davis. Dodgers manager Tommy Lasorda sent Gibson up as a pinch-hitter. Even on

Dodgers slugger Kirk Gibson celebrates as he circles the bases in Game 1 of the 1988 World Series.

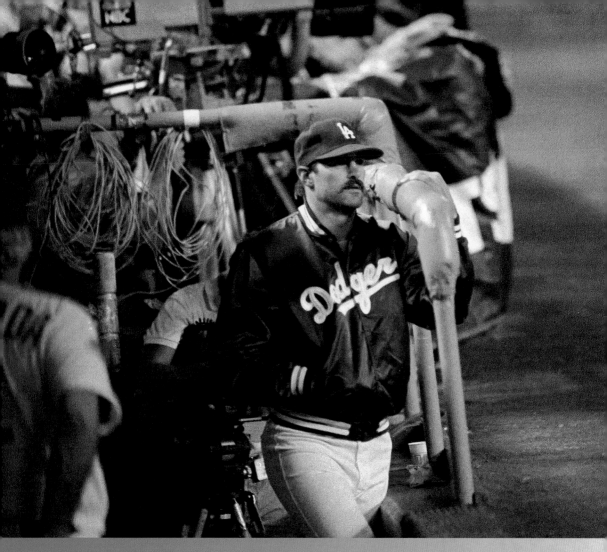

Injuries kept Kirk Gibson on the bench for most of the 1988 World Series.

two bum legs, the 1988 NL MVP was the Dodgers' best chance.

Gibson barely fouled off two pitches. Then he worked the count full. On Eckersley's next pitch,

Gibson swung and the ball jumped off his bat. It landed in the right field seats. Gibson hobbled around the bases, pumping his arms in celebration. The Dodgers had an improbable 5–4 victory.

Los Angeles came into the series as heavy underdogs against the A's, who had won 104 games in the regular season. But the Dodgers won the series in five games.

PHILLY FALLS SHORT

The 1914 Philadelphia Athletics were trying to win their fourth World Series in five seasons. They met the NL champion Boston Braves. The AL champion A's had five future Hall of Famers. The Braves had been 15 games out of first place before storming back to win the NL pennant. However, Boston beat the A's in a four-game sweep.

9

2000 SUMMER OLYMPICS

GARDNER GRABS GOLD

Aleksandr Karelin was called the Siberian Bear. He certainly was as tough as one. The Russian wrestler had not lost a match in 13 years. He owned three Olympic gold medals.

At the 2000 Olympic Games in Sydney, Australia, Karelin faced an unknown farm boy from Wyoming. Rulon Gardner was the youngest of nine children. His farm work was part of his training. Gardner was strong, and he was willing. But could he beat a man who had not given up a point in the previous six years?

Gardner knew his only chance was to score early on Karelin in the super heavyweight final. Thirty seconds into the second round, Gardner broke Karelin's grip during a hold. That gave the American a

Russia's Aleksandr Karelin, *left*, tries to fend off US wrestler Rulon Gardner in the 2000 Olympics.

point. There were still 5 1/2 minutes left. But Gardner's footwork and strength held off the Russian.

With a few seconds remaining, Karelin simply dropped his hands at his side in defeat. After Gardner's hand was raised for his shocking victory, he did a cartwheel and a somersault on the mat. Then he grabbed an American flag and ran through the arena in celebration. Back home in Wyoming, a banner was raised. It said: "Home of Rulon Gardner, Olympic Gold Medalist."

10

2007 FIESTA BOWL
BIG-PLAY BOISE

Boise State had finally crashed the party. The Idaho school had dominated its small conference for years. But the Broncos kept getting invited to play in minor bowl games. That finally changed. The 2006 Broncos turned a 12–0 record into an invitation to a New Year's Day bowl game. Then they turned the game into a huge upset of mighty Oklahoma.

Boise jumped to leads of 14–0 and 28–10 at the Fiesta Bowl. But the more experienced Sooners rallied. They tied the game, then took a 35–28 lead on a late interception return for a touchdown. The clock was about to strike midnight on the Broncos.

Boise State's Jerard Rabb dives into the end zone to score the game-tying touchdown in the 2007 Fiesta Bowl.

Ian Johnson, *left*, takes a sneak handoff from quarterback Jared Zabransky on the final play of the 2007 Fiesta Bowl.

But as the game clock ticked down to zero, the Broncos got creative. Quarterback Jared Zabransky threw a pass over the middle. Receiver Drisan James caught it. Then he flipped it back to teammate Jerard Rabb, who sprinted down the opposite sideline. The 50-yard "hook-and-lateral" play tied the game.

In overtime Oklahoma scored on its first play. Boise State got the ball but soon faced fourth down. It was time for another trick play. The Broncos scored on a wide receiver reverse-option pass.

But they were not done with their trickery. The Broncos went for two. Running back Ian Johnson took a behind-the-back handoff from Zabransky. The "Statue of Liberty" play fooled the Sooners. Johnson ran untouched into the end zone for a 43–42 victory.

Johnson then ran to the sideline, got down on a knee, and proposed to his cheerleader girlfriend. She said yes. It was a fairy-tale ending for a true Cinderella story.

BIG HOUSE BLUES

Big Ten football power Michigan figured to have an easy 2007 opener against tiny Appalachian State. But the fifth-ranked Wolverines discovered they could not handle the Mountaineers' speed or trick plays. Appalachian State blocked a last-second field goal attempt for a 34–32 win. It was the first time a team ranked in the Top 25 had lost to a lower-division opponent.

2008 SUPER BOWL
NOBODY'S PERFECT

In the Super Bowl era, the 1972 Miami Dolphins were the only team to finish a season undefeated. Then came the high-flying 2007 New England Patriots. They swept through 16 regular-season games and won two more in the playoffs.

But to go down in history with the '72 Dolphins, the Patriots still had one more game to win. They faced the New York Giants in the Super Bowl. New England had beaten the Giants in the last game of the regular season. New York slipped into the playoffs as the last seed, then won three road games to get to the Super Bowl.

Defensive end Michael Strahan and his teammates made life miserable for Patriots quarterback Tom Brady.

Giants receiver David Tyree, *left*, pins the ball against his helmet as New England safety Rodney Harrison tries to break up the pass.

New England was a 12-point favorite. With MVP Tom Brady throwing to record-setting receiver Randy Moss, the Patriots looked unstoppable. But the Giants had a plan that had worked throughout the playoffs: get pressure on the quarterback. Every time Brady dropped back to pass, he was rushed heavily. He was sacked five times and hit nine more.

Still, the Patriots went ahead 14–10 late in the fourth quarter. One more defensive stand and they would be champions. The Giants faced third-and-5 from their own 44. The Patriots put heavy pressure on quarterback Eli Manning. But somehow Manning escaped and heaved the ball into the air.

Giants receiver David Tyree caught only four passes during the regular season. But that did not matter. He leaped in the air and pinned the ball against his helmet with one hand as he was falling. The miracle put the Giants deep in New England territory. Four plays later, wide receiver Plaxico Burress caught a 13-yard touchdown pass from Manning. New York won 17–14, and the Patriots' perfect season went up in smoke.

12

2009 PGA

YANG TAMES TIGER

For years Tiger Woods was unbeatable when he led a major championship heading into the final round. He was 14–0 when that happened. Woods also had never lost any tournament on the Professional Golfers Association (PGA) Tour when leading by more than one shot after the third round.

But all that changed at the 2009 PGA Championship at Hazeltine National in Minnesota. In the final round, Woods discovered that he not only had a challenger—he had a conqueror.

Y. E. Yang of South Korea was a little-known golfer going into the PGA Championship. But that weekend, he made a name for himself against the best golfers in the world. Woods entered play on Sunday leading

Y. E. Yang, *left*, shocked the golf world with his victory over Tiger Woods, *right*, in the 2009 PGA Championship.

by two shots. But when Yang chipped in from 60 feet for an eagle on the 14th hole, he took the lead.

On the 18th hole, Yang still led by one stroke. His approach shot from behind a tree soared over a sand trap and onto the green. It rolled to a stop just eight feet from the cup. It was more than Woods could overcome.

Yang tapped in his putt and won by three shots. He became the first Asian player to win a major title on the men's tour.

13

2011 DAYTONA 500
ROOKIE SURPRISE

NASCAR opens its season with the Daytona 500. It is the biggest event of the NASCAR season. Race cars zip around Florida's Daytona International Speedway at speeds topping 200 miles per hour (322 kmh).

Nearly all the greats of stock car racing have won the Great American Race. Those who have not consider it a career goal. Meanwhile, Trevor Bayne turned 20 the day before the 500 in 2011. He was not even a regular in the Sprint Cup series. For Bayne, happiness was simply getting a chance to race at Daytona.

Then something odd happened. Bayne's car was so fast that he was near the lead with a handful of

Trevor Bayne is all smiles at the Daytona International Speedway.

laps to go. Stars such as Tony Stewart, Dale Earnhardt Jr., and Mark Martin chased him. But Bayne kept his foot down and his car in front. He took the checkered flag, giving his team owners the Wood Brothers their first win in 10 years.

Then Bayne finally messed up. He was so excited that he missed the turn into Victory Lane.

HONORABLE MENTIONS

Navy beats Army, 1950—Navy hadn't beaten archrival Army in football since 1943, and this matchup didn't look promising: Army was 8–0, Navy was 2–6. Yet the Midshipmen won 14–2.

New York Giants over Cleveland Indians, 1954—Cleveland won a record 111 games in the AL and was an overwhelming choice to beat New York in the World Series. Instead the Giants, led by future Hall of Fame center fielder Willie Mays, swept four games.

Villanova beats Georgetown, 1985—Top-ranked Georgetown was the defending NCAA men's basketball champion. Villanova was unranked. But the Wildcats made 22 of 28 shots in the national championship game, shocking the mighty Hoyas 66–64.

Michael Chang, 1989—Chang beat the world's top tennis player, Ivan Lendl, then stunned third-seeded Stefan Edberg to become the first American since 1955 to win the French Open.

Douglas over Tyson, 1990—Mike Tyson was the heavyweight boxing champion and the most feared man in the sport. He entered the bout against unheralded Buster Douglas with a 37–0 record. But Douglas, a 42-to-1 underdog, controlled the fight from the start and knocked out Tyson in the tenth round.

Duke beats UNLV, 1991—UNLV crushed Duke in the 1990 NCAA men's basketball title game. The next year, Duke turned it around. UNLV was 34–0, but Duke won 79–77 in the NCAA semifinals.

Adelina Sotnikova, 2014—Julia Lipnitskaya was the Russian darling in figure skating at the Winter Olympics in Sochi. But Sotnikova surprised everyone, edging defending champion Kim Yuna of South Korea for the gold medal.

GLOSSARY

amateurs
Athletes who are not paid to play their sport.

bout
A fight in boxing or wrestling.

checkered flag
The flag waved when the winning car crosses the finish line at the end of a car race.

clutch
Able to succeed in important situations.

eagle
In golf, two shots below the expected score, or par, for a hole.

furlong
One-eighth of a mile.

heavyweight
The heaviest weight class in wrestling and boxing.

tournament
An event held to decide a champion.

underdogs
The team or athlete expected to lose a competition.

FOR MORE INFORMATION

Books

Berman, Len. *The Greatest Moments in Sports: Upsets and Underdogs.* Naperville, IL: Sourcebooks, 2012.

Rappoport, Ken. *Biggest Upsets in Sports.* Minneapolis, MN, Abdo Publishing, 2013.

Spizman, Justin, and Robyn Spizman. *Don't Give Up . . . Don't Ever Give Up: The Inspiration of Jimmy V.* Naperville, IL: Sourcebooks, 2010.

Websites

To learn more about the Legendary World of Sports, visit **booklinks.abdopublishing.com.** These links are routinely monitored and updated to provide the most current information available.

INDEX

ABOUT THE AUTHOR

Barry Wilner has been a sportswriter for the Associated Press since 1976 and has covered World Cups, Super Bowls, the Olympics, and many other sporting events. He also has written more than 50 books, and he teaches sports journalism at Manhattanville College. He lives with his wife in Garnerville, New York.